6 Vols.

LEXILE
230 - 270

JMP
Ti

Construction Zone

Publisher: **Jump!, Inc. / Bullfrog Books**
Library Binding   AU(Rebecca Pettiford)

Gumdrop Price $113.70
Publisher's List Price $161.94

Do you have readers who just can't get enough of big machines? Vibrant photographs of large construction vehicles at work, photo labels and diagrams work together with tightly controlled vocabulary to make this a fun and exciting series for beginning readers. Each title includes reading tips for teachers and parents, a table of contents and a glossary and index.

Additional Series :
- JMP0400 English
- JMP0414 Spanish
- JMP0415 Spanish

eBook
Library Binding eBook

	Title	Dewey	©	Price
Le	Backhoes	621.8	23	$18.95
Le	Bulldozers SK	629.2	23	$18.95
Le	Concrete Mixers	620.1	23	$18.95
Le	Cranes SK	621.8	23	$18.95
Le	Diggers	621.8	23	$18.95
Le	Rollers SK	625.7	23	$18.95

GD FIELD : 8/15/2023 (6x5½)   USD
Page 1 of 1   Titles may be purchased individually.

Need for Speed

Rally Cars

by Bizzy Harris

Bullfrog Books

Ideas for Parents and Teachers

Bullfrog Books let children practice reading informational text at the earliest reading levels. Repetition, familiar words, and photo labels support early readers.

Before Reading
- Discuss the cover photo. What does it tell them?
- Look at the picture glossary together. Read and discuss the words.

Read the Book
- "Walk" through the book and look at the photos. Let the child ask questions. Point out the photo labels.
- Read the book to the child, or have him or her read independently.

After Reading
- Prompt the child to think more. Ask: Rally cars race on many different surfaces. Where did you see rally cars race in this book?

Bullfrog Books are published by Jump!
5357 Penn Avenue South
Minneapolis, MN 55419
www.jumplibrary.com

Copyright © 2023 Jump! International copyright reserved in all countries. No part of this book may be reproduced in any form without written permission from the publisher.

Library of Congress Cataloging-in-Publication Data

Names: Harris, Bizzy, author.
Title: Rally cars / by Bizzy Harris.
Description: Minneapolis, MN: Jump!, Inc., [2023]
Series: Need for speed| Includes index.
Audience: Ages 5–8
Identifiers: LCCN 2021044315 (print)
LCCN 2021044316 (ebook)
ISBN 9781636906782 (hardcover)
ISBN 9781636906799 (paperback)
ISBN 9781636906805 (ebook)
Subjects: LCSH: Rally cars—Juvenile literature.
Classification: LCC TL236.4 .H37 2023 (print)
LCC TL236.4 (ebook) | DDC 796.7/3—dc23
LC record available at
https://lccn.loc.gov/2021044315
LC ebook record available at
https://lccn.loc.gov/2021044316

Editor: Eliza Leahy
Designer: Emma Bersie

Photo Credits: Rodrigo Garrido/Shutterstock, cover, 24; EvrenKalinbacak/Shutterstock, 1, 4, 13; Babeshkin/Shutterstock, 3; Taras Vyshnya/Shutterstock, 5; Johner Images/Alamy, 6–7, 23bm; mountainpix/Shutterstock, 8–9, 23bl; Ermess/Dreamstime, 10–11; Aurelian Nedelcu/Shutterstock, 12, 23tm; Action Plus Sports Images/Alamy, 14–15, 20–21; Anadolu Agency/Getty, 16–17; Weblogiq/Dreamstime, 18, 23tr; Zigmunds Dizgalvis/iStock, 19, 23br; coffeeflavour/Shutterstock, 22 (top); MRYsportfoto/Shutterstock, 22 (bottom); Manamana/Shutterstock, 23tl.

Printed in the United States of America at Corporate Graphics in North Mankato, Minnesota.

Table of Contents

Mud and Ice	4
Parts of a Rally Car	22
Picture Glossary	23
Index	24
To Learn More	24

Mud and Ice

A rally car races.
It drives through mud!

One person drives.

He makes a sharp turn!

headset

The other person gives directions.

They both wear headsets.

Why?

The car is loud!

driver

Both wear helmets.

Harnesses hold them in.

helmet

harness

roll cage

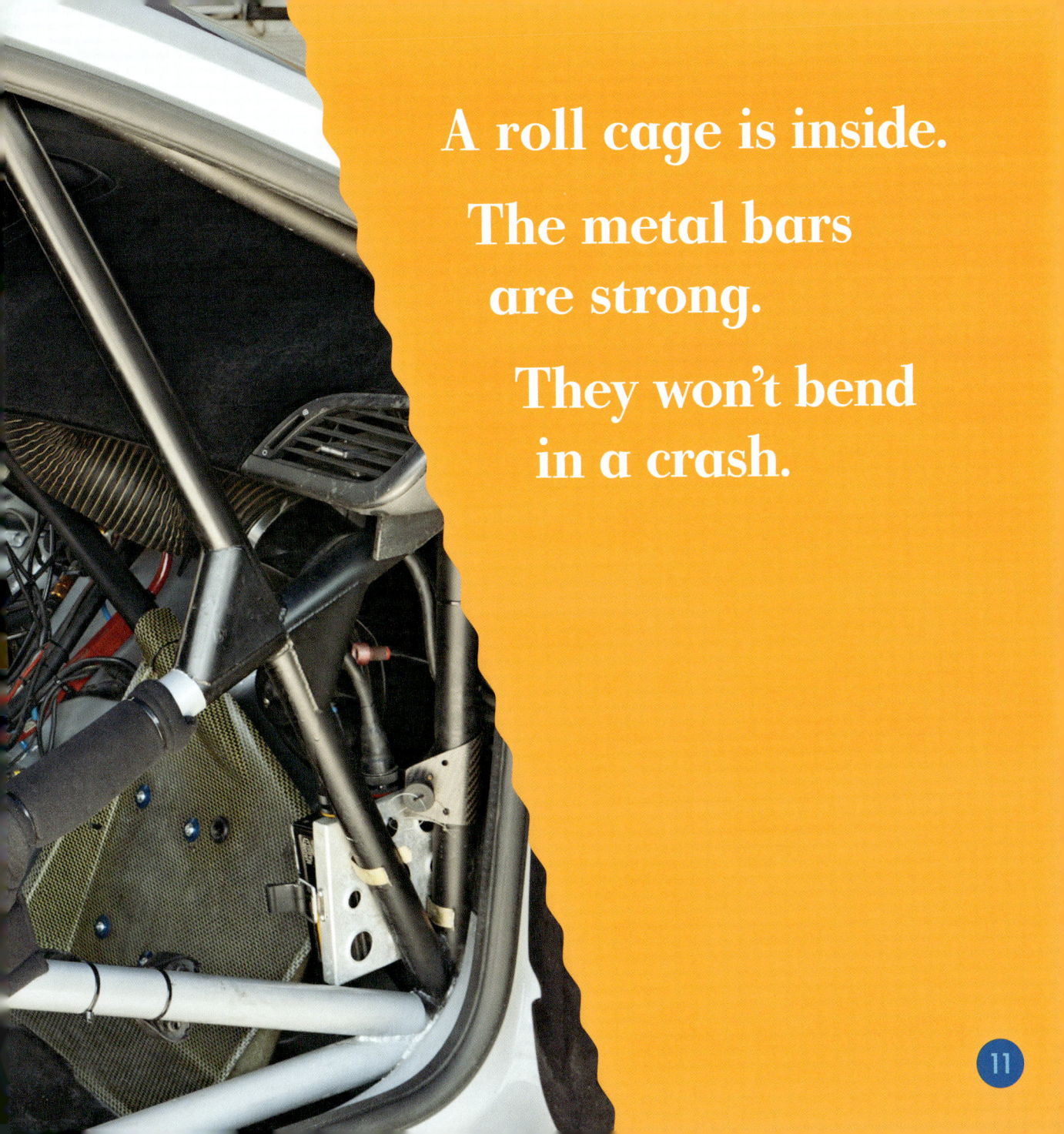

A roll cage is inside. The metal bars are strong. They won't bend in a crash.

Rally cars drive on gravel roads.

gravel

dirt

They drive on dirt trails, too.

This car goes over a jump.
It gets air!

15

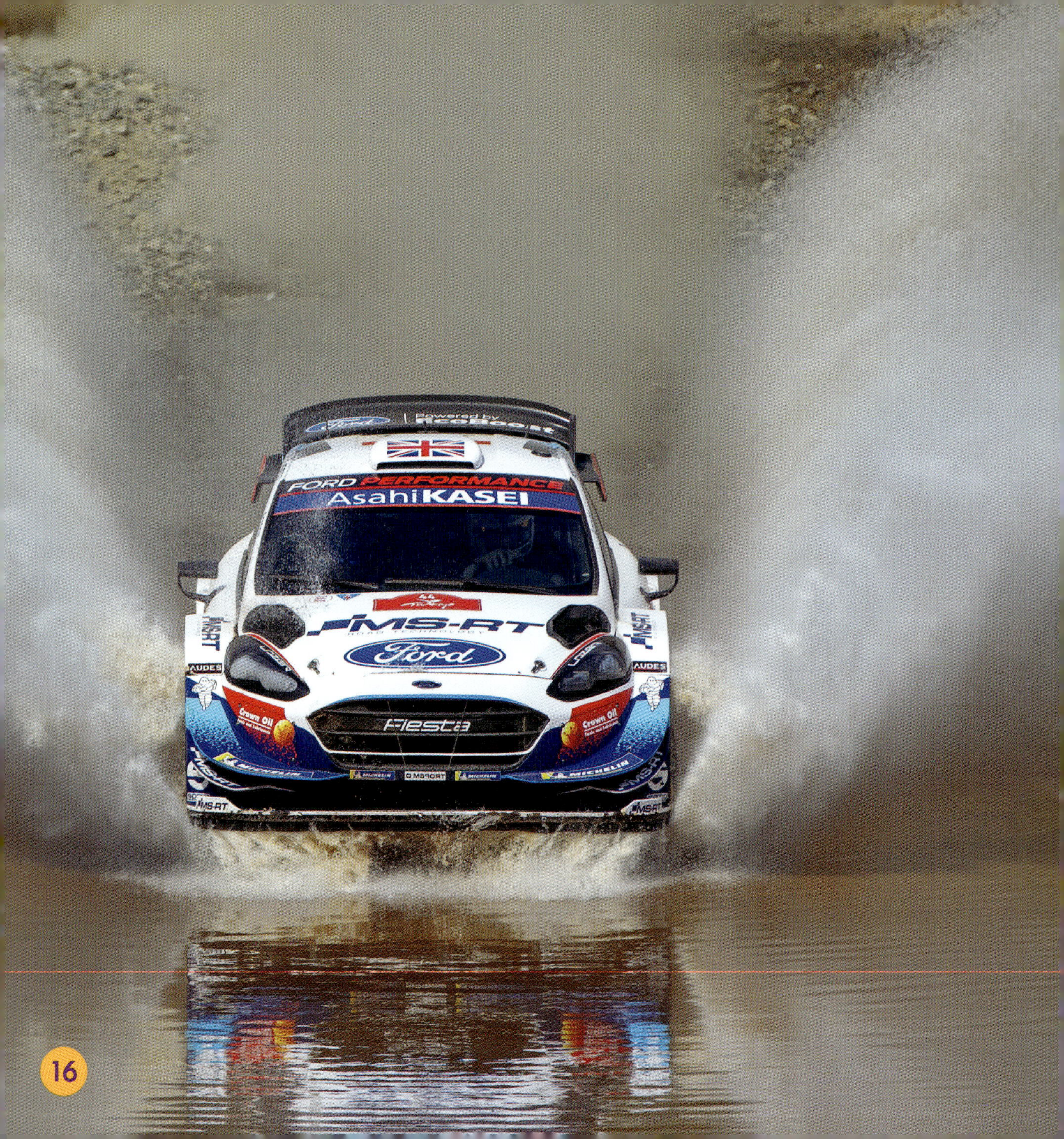
FORD PERFORMANCE
AsahiKASEI
MS-RT
Ford
Fiesta
Crown Oil

This one crosses a river.
Splash!

This car races in snow.

The tires have studs.
They grip ice.

stud

Races are long.
They can last days.
One car races at a time.
The fastest time wins!

finish line

Parts of a Rally Car

A rally car can go 130 miles (209 kilometers) per hour. Take a look at its parts!

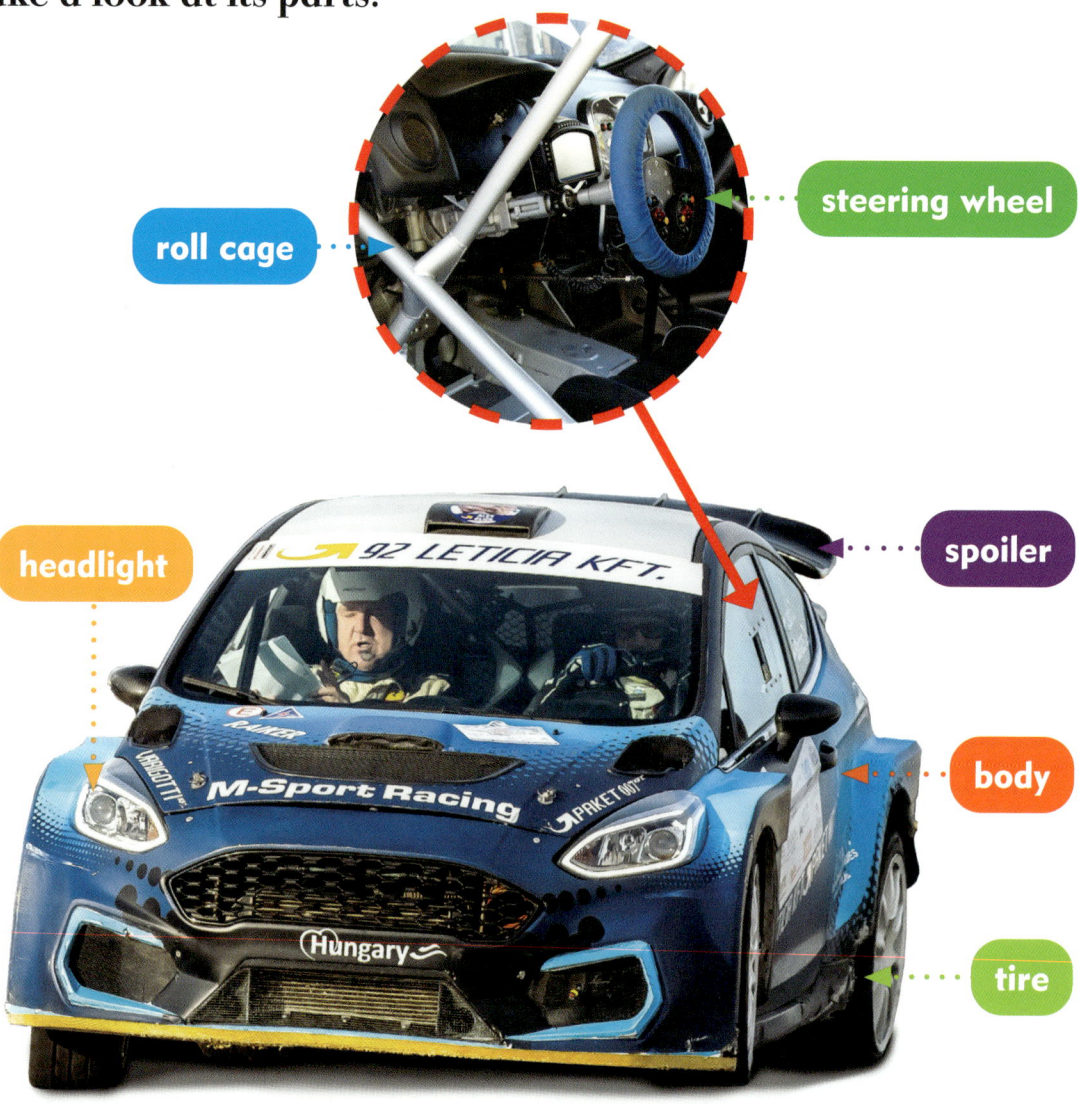

roll cage

steering wheel

headlight

spoiler

body

tire

Picture Glossary

directions
Instructions, especially for getting somewhere.

gravel
A loose mixture of small stones used on paths or roads.

grip
To keep a tight hold on something.

harnesses
Sets of straps used to connect you to something and keep you safe.

headsets
Devices that hold headphones and microphones on peoples' heads.

studs
Metal cleats used on tires for better grip.

Index

drives 4, 5, 12, 13
harnesses 8
headsets 7
helmets 8
ice 19
jump 14
mud 4
races 4, 18, 20
river 17
roll cage 11
snow 18
tires 19

To Learn More

Finding more information is as easy as 1, 2, 3.

❶ Go to www.factsurfer.com

❷ Enter "rallycars" into the search box.

❸ Choose your book to see a list of websites.